us & them

us & them

bridging the chasm of faith

w.c. scheurer

Requests for permission to make copies of any part of
this work should be mailed to the following address:
W.C. Scheurer, P.O. Box 132, Antioch, IL 60002-0132; or
sent by email to publisher@hourglassbooks.com

Cover Artwork by Randi Layne Scheurer
www.randiworks.com

ISBN 0-9725254-1-6
LCCN 2003116862

Printed in the United States of America
on acid-free paper

Published by Hourglass Books
www.hourglassbooks.com

On behalf of InterfaithJourney
www.interfaithjourney.com

Chapter One
Faith

This is a book about faith, yours and mine, ours and theirs, us and them. Our defining faiths bring us together. They also keep us apart, often with tragic consequences. My hope in writing this is to make some small contribution toward changing this unnecessary result.

Faith

This book is written mainly with believers in mind, people who practice a religion, especially those who may feel sharply divided from others who do not believe the same things as them. If you are not such a believer, please do not feel left out. Perhaps you will find something in these pages that suggests a different approach to religion than that which you have found lacking so far.

Before we go on, let me say that I claim no special qualifications as a religious teacher. These words are simply a fruition of conscience and belief, and are shared with you as that and nothing more.

The observations in this book are based on a lifetime of study and practice in faith (including lessons learned from many mistakes), which has nourished an ever-growing sense of gratitude for the ever-present love of God. Its writing is impelled by the sad circumstance that many people of deep faith (who also have shared the same experience of this love) are still at tragic odds with each other after so many centuries of coexistence.

One thing I have come to firmly grasp is that this is not what God wants from believers. Rather, as believers (of all people), we should accept and respect the faith of others, as genuinely valid as our own. If we do not, we tend to invalidate our own faith, since all of us are human and subject to the same limitations.

Faith

It is possible for sincere believers to achieve a unity of faith while cherishing our diversity of practice and belief. All believers in God share the same experience—that of genuine faith. In fact, all people share in this predicament of faith, whether they believe in God or not. It is simply a matter of where we place our faith, and how we perceive the nature of reality. We all form beliefs in this world where we live without perfect knowledge.

Faith is a principle of action and understanding in a world we do not fully comprehend. It is a blend of thought, feeling, will and response to God and the mystery of life. Faith is how we live in this world. We place our faith in many things.

Wake up in the morning. Get out of bed. Walk out the door. These all are supreme acts of faith. We need faith in an outcome to give us the will to act. Without this power of faith, we can do nothing. With faith, is how we do everything. How then can we ever place our faith above another's? They are the same. Because we do not have a perfect knowledge of reality, we all must live by faith.

Chapter Two
Diversity

As with many things in life, we articulate our initial ideas about the being and nature of God in terms that we first received from others as we were growing up. We form ideas about God, like we form ideas about a chair, a cat, or any other thing, and these ideas develop throughout our lives as we grow in experience.

Diversity

Throughout this process, the shared specifics of our languages are (in large part) social skills, and most (if not all) of our concepts are tagged with shared meaning.

In the case of religious faith, the force of shared meaning is even more specific. As believers, we are given testimonies, teachings, stories and histories from those who bring us into the faith and offer continued support and guidance there. These bodies of scripture and canon form the basis of our shared beliefs.

It is in this context that we begin to have our own approaches to Divinity, as our religious life moves from that of received ideas to deeply experienced belief and living faith. As a consequence, we feel a strong bond of loyalty, trust and gratitude toward those teachings, leaders, traditions and communities that helped foster these experiences in our lives.

These feelings also give us a strong sense of "us," belonging to a community of believers who share in our perception and understanding of God. In its benign aspect, this feeling of belonging is deeply gratifying and helps sustain our vital faith.

However, there also can be a negative potential to these emotions, when our sense of "us" closes in and leads to a counterbalancing sense of "them," those who do not share our precise beliefs and practices. To give way to this tendency is to deny our

Diversity

faith. Instead of living in the humility of faith, we arrogate to ourselves the knowledge of God. Who among us can claim a perfect knowledge?

We need to understand and truly accept that people who believe differently from us have shared the same experience of faith as we have. They have the same bonds of loyalty and gratitude to their teachers and fellow believers, the same sense of "us," as we have in our faith.

Does this faith of others who have different practices and beliefs make "them" *less* like "us" or *more*? The very fact that they also believe in God with the same deep devotion as we do, and grow a living faith based on their own spiritual experiences in the context of their specific religious traditions like we do, makes us more alike. God is the same, for us as for them. Our faith is the same. The only thing that is different is the way each group has learned to practice its faith and comprehend its beliefs.

Chapter Three
Humility

There is a well-known story about blind men and an elephant. One man grabs hold of its ear and says that an elephant is like a soft, leathery fan. Another grabs hold of its tail and says an elephant is like a thick, coarse rope. A third grabs its tusk and says an elephant is like a smooth, sharp spear. Another grabs its trunk and says an elephant is like a pliant hose. The last man holds on to its leg and says that an elephant is like a firm pillar. Of course, they all believe they are right and the others are wrong about the elephant.

The story goes on to note the seeing man who tells them that they all are right and all are wrong about the elephant. It is all of these things, and more. A likeness then is drawn between our conceptions about God and reality and the blind men's ideas about the nature of an elephant.

An interesting and helpful story. Yet, in its telling and hearing, there is always a presumption that the tellers and hearers are more like the sighted man who sees the whole picture, and that others are like the blind men who cling to the error of their dogmatic beliefs. But, it might be equally useful to think of all of us as being blind, in the sense that none of us at present fully comprehends the nature and being of God.

Let's play with this parable a bit more. To see something as big as an elephant, you would need to step away from it—let go of it. Its majesty is so great that we could never see it all and hold on to it at the same time, in our current perspective. Is it better to see a true picture of the Divine, or to hold on to (embrace) a living God in faith and love? Which experience gives us more joy and life?

Humility

Of course, this is just a story, ideas and words. But, in a very real sense, so are our doctrines about the nature of God, ideas and words. Are the beliefs of a blind man holding on to an elephant's ear any more or less valid than the beliefs of a blind man holding on to its tail? They both feel the elephant as a living being.

God is a living reality to all believers. We know what Divine love feels like, and we can describe it with reference to other life experiences, in the terms of our own faiths. Does this concrete conviction of ours negate the like conviction of theirs? Do we know God in some way other than through the exercise of faith, sustained by our spiritual experience of God's love?

Humility

The faith of all believers is the same. It is the key means of approach by humanity to God. What is more important? This shared experience of the love of God, or our different ways of understanding and expressing this experience among our religions? Can any of us truly apprehend or describe the majesty of God, by means of our limited human ideas and words?

Chapter Four
Religion

If the faith of all believers is the same, does this mean all religions are the same? Not at all.

Each one is distinct, and the followers of each religion concretely believe in its teachings, since this is where our exercise of faith has been validated by the tangible experience of God's love. In this way, we each form an understandable conviction that our religion is true.

These convictions form the core around which fall into place all the scriptures, revelations, teachings, beliefs and practices that contain the specifics of our diverse religions. We know that God loves us. We come to know this by our faith.

In the joy and passion of this personal conviction, further charged by the exhilaration of sharing it with others in our religious community, it is easy for us to overlook the fact that people who belong to different faiths also share this experience, the same as us. They also know their religions are true. God tells them.

Religion

If this is so, does it matter what religion we practice, or even whether we have one at all? Yes, it matters a great deal to us, since we believe the things we do. Just as it matters to them, since they believe the things they do. Who can tell us our faith is not true? God's love has validated it. By the same token, who can tell them their faith is not true? God's love has validated it.

How is it possible to hold these two seemingly contradictory realizations at once, the knowledge that our religion is true to us, and that their religion is true to them, without denying or devaluing our own faith? The key is humility. In fact, humility further validates our faith, when we see others in diverse circumstances repeat the experience of God's love by faith. In respecting the truths of other faiths, we respect the truth of our own.

So, if it matters to us which religion we follow, does it matter to God? That is a question only God can answer for each individual. But, what does seem clear from careful study of nearly every religion is that it matters to God *how* we practice our religions, whichever they may be.

At the common core of every faith is love—our feeling of worship for God, and our care for each other. This is something that every religion holds as its highest value, the central thrust of all its teaching.

Religion

Given this commonality of message in every religion, in view of all our differences in specific details of practice and belief, it is clear that God is trying to tell us what is most important—that we love. In light of God's known love for us, this gives meaning to the ideas of humankind being made in the image of God, of us being children of God.

Chapter Five
Worship

When we feel God's love for us, our reaction is to love back. But the power of God's love is so great, and our corresponding feelings are also so strong, that we need another word to describe it.

Worship is the love we give back toward a love that we perceive is overwhelming compared to ours.

Worship

Worship is our love of God. It gives rise to the strongest feelings known to us in this life, and is attended by feelings of awe and gratitude. People of all religions know this feeling, as do people who sense the power and love of God by other means.

If this experience sounds foreign to you, be assured, it is not. Everyone who lives knows this love. We could not live without it.

As faith is our means—how we live, love is our motive—why we live. All people feel this human need, to love and to be loved.

This love is the same for everyone, "us" and "them." We all live by it the same. Only our beliefs

Worship

and practices differ from each other, how we learn to live this love.

The underlying motivation, love of God, is the same. Even with the outward differences in forms of practice and belief, we share a same fundamental sense of what it means to do good, to love and care for each other, especially those in need.

This is the vital core of all our teachings, to love God by loving each other. Everything else is secondary to this, as all our faiths proclaim. This is what it means to worship God.

What is more important? Our differences in practice and belief, or these feelings of worship and love that we all share? Does this love by others who have different practices

23

and beliefs make "them" *less* like "us" or *more*? The very fact that they also worship God as we do, and try to love one another as we do, makes us more alike. This worship and love are the same, for us as for them. The only thing different is the way each group learns to express and practice this calling of worship and love.

Loving one another is key. If we fail in this, we fail in our worship of God. If we fail to see the image of God in any of the children of God, we fail to see God in that instance. When we see this image, we see God.

This is one of the main ways God has given us to see the Divine in this life, reflected in one another. This is so for "us" as it is for "them." Each

24

person is a child of God. If not, who else put them here? Is there any God but God, some other giver of life?

If we revere the worship in other faiths different from ours, we revere our own. If we disrespect this worship because of its differences, we deny our own faith, disrespecting the love of God by our own siblings, who come to know this love through faith, the same way we come to know it.

Chapter Six
Evil

Often, our human need for love becomes twisted and acted out in negative ways. We see this in cases of crime, religious persecution, racial hatred and other destructive behavior by human beings. What we refer to as "evil" is the painful result.

This condition exists in all of us in varying degrees and in different ways from time to time. However, we seldom see it in ourselves.

This is the biggest problem with evil, that we see it in others but not ourselves. Whenever we do evil, we have our justification. It is always someone else who is at fault. The evil is not in "us" but in "them."

There is a benign reason for this as well. We all value the idea of "good," and like to see ourselves as committed to good. We need this to keep our feelings of self-worth.

However, this also has the negative effect of blinding us to the evil in ourselves. This is not a vague notion of evil in the sense that we all have faults and no one is perfect. It is much more. We are complicit in real evil in this world, the kind that hurts others and destroys lives.

We do not intend to do this evil, and do not recognize we do it, but we all do it in one way or other. This is what our faiths are all about, to help lead us from this evil, to lead us into greater good.

When we deny this evil, we therefore deny our faith, our need to reduce the evil and increase the good in ourselves as our daily task. We fail to recognize the majesty of God as the epitome of all that is good and falsely arrogate pure goodness to ourselves. To fully appreciate the love of God it is important for us to truly recognize how far we are now from having this perfect love ourselves.

Evil

The basic nature of evil is always the same. Evil is when we deny the worth of another human being as equal in value to our own, whether in matters of pleasure and pain, life and death, freedom and bondage, or personal status. In the context of individuals, evil is acted out between "you" and "me." In the context of groups, it is between "us" and "them." But the root is the same, the feeling that I am more important than you, "us" more than "them."

Evil is at its greatest when these feelings are directed toward those we define as our enemy. Here we demonize the enemy, positing all evil in them, arrogating all good to ourselves. It becomes a clear case of right and wrong, black and white, good and evil, "us" and "them." We deny the reality of God (even while invoking God for our cause), as we declare ourselves to be God instead, the reservoir of all that is good.

The evil we see in our enemy is in us. The good we see in ourselves is in our enemy. When we lose sight of this, we lose sight of God, and then we commit our most evil deeds.

Chapter Seven
Conscience

Conscience is how we tell good from evil. It is part of us being made in the image of God, as God's children. Our conscience is one of the most deeply personal components of our beings, something we treasure as an integral part of who we are.

Although it has this deeply personal side, conscience is largely a social phenomenon, just as good and evil are social (based on how we treat each other). We form our conscience through interaction with others, from seeing how others (whom we love or from whom we seek love) in a group react to our actions.

This growth of conscience takes place within such groups as families, neighborhoods, religious institutions, schools, and elsewhere, as our lives become more involved with other people and we see how our actions affect them.

If we limit this concern for others to members of our own small group ("us"), we limit the formation of our conscience. As we extend our concern to include people from other groups ("them"), we further develop our conscience. This leads to greater tolerance, understanding and respect on our part for the beliefs, practices, values and needs of others.

If we narrowly constrain our conscience to the values of the small groups to which we belong, we will not know how to choose good when we encounter others outside of these groups who present different needs and values to us. If our conscience is alive and growing, open to the equal worth and dignity of all other people, we will know how to see the good in "them" and the evil in "us," and will be able to hone our conscience rather than dull it by the encounter.

Conscience

We all have conscience, the ability to see God's image in others. Because we have this, we feel good about our values and ourselves; we feel we know right from wrong. But, we can easily forget that others have this too, and also feel that they know right from wrong, have learned it in their groups as we have in ours.

Just as our conscience is informed by groups, it can also be malformed by them. We can easily see this in gangs and tribes where criminal conspiracy or genocide is supported by group loyalties.

Here again, it is less easy to recognize this same group dynamic at work in our own lives. But every time we commit evil (fail to equally

Conscience

value the worth of another person),
we find ourselves justifying it with
reference to our family, our nation,
our company, or some other group
whose needs and regards are more
important to "us" than "them."

Each time we recognize the
image of God in God's children and
respond with a love that our worship
of God impels, our conscience grows.
This is especially so when we see it in
"them" that are less like "us."

Chapter Eight
Killing

One of the worst evils we can ever do is to kill another person. This denies the equal value of someone to such an extent that we judge him not worthy even to exist.

Killing also arrogates to us a false sense of the power of God, that over life itself. Since we cannot create life, the next most powerful deed is to destroy it. If our need for love gets so twisted, that we deny the right to life of another being, we have gone very far from seeing God.

When we see God's image in others, we could never destroy them, except perhaps in a most drastic case where it is necessary to stop someone from imminently destroying another, which is extremely rare.

To go beyond such cases in abstractions and policies that justify the killing of others for such reasons as retaliation, preemption, justice, or other concepts, is to elevate our ideas (which are in some sense "us") above the value of another being (an enemy, a criminal, etc., "them").

Killing

To do this would be saying that, because someone has done (or possibly may do) great wrong, they are no longer children of God, made in the image of God, of equal worth and dignity as ourselves.

It is a failure to recognize the evil that is in "us," and the good that is still in "them," a failure to see God, just like what we accuse the guilty of doing. Then we arrogate to ourselves a pale imitation of the power of God, to destroy what we cannot create.

One of the worst forms of killing is war. It is organized killing carried out on a massive scale. It also is extreme group behavior based on an abstraction, an extreme collective sense of "us" and "them." In war, we set out to kill entire groups of people who are unknown to us. War denies our humanity on all sides. In acts of war, we fail to see the image of God in an entire population, we suspend our consciences to the mass hysteria of an entire group that arrogates the goodness of God to itself ("us") and denies it in others ("them").

When we so deeply separate ourselves ("us") from recognizing the image of God in others ("them") as to kill strangers for abstract reasons, we deeply separate ourselves from God. This is why political leaders and their followers so much invoke the support of God for their side in a war, because it is a time when we are furthest from God and our own conscience. This is also why we do the most horrible evil deeds in war, like genocidal attacks on noncombatants and destruction of the civil fabric of societies, which we always justify as military necessity or collateral damage on both sides of the conflict to assuage our guilt.

God does not want us to kill one another. In a rare case where we believe we must defend another, then let us act in full humility. Who are we to claim God is on our side?

Chapter Nine
Humiliation

If killing, destroying another human being in the image of God, is one of the most evil acts we can ever do, then humiliation, destroying the self-esteem of another human being, may be the next closest thing.

As killing destroys the body, life itself, so humiliation destroys the psyche, the will to live. It also denies the basic worth of another person, as someone not worthy of respect.

If we see the image of God in others, as children of God, we cannot cause humiliation to them. In fact, we can only have the utmost respect and humility before them, no matter how they may differ from us. If we do not feel this, it is a sign of our separation from God, our failure to see the love of God in the image of others.

Just as war is killing at its worst, so persecution and prejudice are humiliation at its worst. They are conspiracies to inflict humiliation on groups of people ("them") unknown to the perpetrators ("us"), for the sole reason that they are different from us in some way that challenges our own sense of personal self-worth.

This is always the cause for humiliation of another, lack of self-worth in ourselves. This in turn is a failure to see the love of God for us, and the image of God in ourselves as children of God. If we cannot see this in ourselves, then we cannot see it in others, and we are distant from God. As we begin to truly accept the love of God for us, we begin to recognize this love for everyone.

The more we accept God's love, the more secure we become of the power of this love to confirm our self-worth, and the less need we feel to falsely compensate for our lack of self-worth by denigrating others. We

Humiliation

see the equal worth of everyone as a
child of God, both those who appear
to be like us, and those who seem to
be different ("them").

Most of the love we know on
this earth comes from others. This is
how we come to appreciate our self-
worth, that others love us. It also is
how we come to know God; the love
that others give us, begins to show
God's love for us.

When we inflict humiliation
on another, we deny this love, both
for ourselves ("us") and for the ones
we humiliate ("them"). In doing this,
we also deny God, who all faiths tell
us is pure love.

Looking back over half a
century of lessons and mistakes, the

only things that truly cause me deep sorrow and regret are times when my actions were part of tearing down the self-esteem of another human being, instead of building them up. It seems like all the other evils I have done in my life are nothing (though they are not) compared to this. These are our most directly personal failings; times when we fail to see the image of God standing right in front of us.

Chapter Ten
Service

If this love of God is not something you have experienced yourself, there is a proven reliable way to cultivate it. Find someone whom you can serve without any thought of return and serve them with humble gratitude.

As you persist in serving others, you will come to know this love. This is a basic teaching of all religions, and has been proven by countless believers over millennia. What we serve, we love.

Service to others is a proven path to God. I have never known or heard of anyone who exercised faith in this principle and did not come to discover a greater love. As we grow in love, we draw closer to God. Our faith teaches us God is love. To learn love for the children of God, is how we learn to know God.

If you work in one of the service occupations, you may feel your work is enough to prove this principle on its own. And, it might. I have met people at their jobs (nurses, janitors, librarians, grocers—to name a few) who radiate this love. People like this are a great joy and comfort wherever we find them.

But this does not mean it will be that way for everyone who works in these fields. When we help others as part of our jobs, it is not always an act of pure service. Sometimes it may simply be trade, what we do to make a living. There is nothing wrong with this. It is all part of life.

But, the service that leads to love of God is when we lose sight of our own interests in caring for those of another. This is pure love of God, to do things for others without any thought for ourselves.

Likewise, parents may often feel their service to their children is enough to prove this principle on its own. Here again, it might. The love between parent and child is perhaps the closest thing on earth to the love of God. This is why people hold this relationship in such high esteem, is why we think of ourselves as being the "children" of God.

If you find such love there, you already know what this means and can relate this experience to the love of God. However, if you do not find the love of God through this, it does not mean you are a bad parent. It simply means you need to look for others to serve to find this love.

Just as in our work, being a parent has many rewards. To belong in a family is deeply gratifying, and to be a key part of that group can be one of the greatest satisfactions we ever find in life. Also, it is common for parents to have expectations for their children that may serve their own needs more than the child's.

If we do not find the love of God at work or home, this is normal. It simply means we need to look for other places to serve. Once found in any place, we find it everywhere.

Chapter Eleven
Compassion

What we sow in service we reap in compassion. As we learn to serve through an exercise of faith, we begin to grow true feelings for others, as children of God like ourselves.

The more we develop these feelings, the more we seek to serve, and it continues in an upward spiral of increased service and love. This is as provable as any experiment. It can be tested by anyone, of any religious belief or lack thereof, with the same results. This is observable fact.

Accepting love is another important part of the equation. It is necessary that we continue to know God's love for us as well, in order to keep the equation in balance.

Think of this not so much as "give and take," but more like "give and accept." Otherwise, it is no more than friendly trade, which in itself is a wonderful part of life but is not the same as selfless love for others.

Compassion has two key elements: 1) a deep awareness of the suffering of others, and 2) a desire to relieve it or share the burden. It is so close to God's love for us that people naturally have deep feelings of warm respect for those who show this trait to a high degree in their lives. We can see the image of God in them.

This is so for a group, as well as an individual. When a group ("us" or "them") shows compassion on the suffering of others, we can see God's love in that group. This is a big factor in the conversion process. People see God's love for them in the group and they want to become part of it. This is as true for other groups ("them") as it is for our own groups ("us"), whether they be religious communities or not, this attraction of love is the same. We belong to many types of groups.

Compassion

The root of compassion is to see others the same way that we see ourselves, the way that God sees all of us, with selfless love. Our love for ourselves (odd as this may sound) is actually a selfless love, since there is no separation between the one who loves and the one who is loved. This is a pure (albeit limited) love.

It is only when others are involved that selfishness can enter the picture. If there is a separation between "us" and "them," then we can begin to prefer ourselves more than another. The challenge and gift of compassion is to love others with the same pure love as ourselves.

As this gift of love grows, we begin to feel the sufferings of others

Compassion

("them") the same as our own ("us"), and we can no longer accept brutish notions such as collateral damage or acceptable losses in war, retribution in criminal justice, or survival of the fittest in economics. Every single life becomes of equal worth to us as our own, every self the same as our own, whether rich or poor, healthy or sick, young or old, believer or nonbeliever, friend or enemy, "us" or "them." We feel their suffering all the same.

Chapter Twelve
Celebration

The other side of compassion is celebration. If we bear the sorrows of others, we also share in their joys. Good that comes to another ("them"), also comes to us the same as our own. We celebrate every good thing.

When we look at others the same as ourselves, good received by them takes nothing away from us, it only adds to our joy. Feelings of envy and spite give way to ones of support and collaboration. We value another's success and benefit ("them") as much as we value our own ("us").

Just as we learn to value the suffering of others the same as our own, so do we value their joy. Their happiness becomes as important to us as our own, when we love others the same as we love ourselves.

Good received by others can never take anything good away from us. It adds to the supply of goodness in the world, not subtracts from it. If we do not celebrate every good thing, we imply that the goodness of God is limited, that there is not enough to go around. This denies God's love.

Celebration

Of course, it can be hard to recognize this, when we feel needs and desires that are not yet filled to our satisfaction. But, that is another issue. The fact remains that the good received by others has nothing to do with the good that remains available to us. It can be especially hard to see this in situations where we compete with others for limited rewards that many of us want. The fact that only few receive these rewards actually has no bearing on the other rewards that are there for us if we search for them with faith in God's love.

Meanwhile, we can rejoice with the joy of others, feeling that all good received by anyone is equal in value to good received by us. When we love others the same as ourselves, all goodness is the same to us.

Is it possible to feel this way? Yes, in fact it is easy. All we need to do is let go of false pride, the foolish belief that our suffering and rewards ("us") are somehow more important than those of others ("them").

When we see God's image in all of God's children, we see them all as worthy of God's love, the same as ourselves. We celebrate the goodness of God toward everyone, the same as when it comes in our direction.

Although it seems harder to us, this celebration is actually easier than compassion. When we learn to share in the joy of others, we add to our own joy. Once we let go of false pride, it becomes easy to feel this joy. It is much more challenging to feel the suffering of others, because it is natural for us to avoid any suffering whenever we can. That is why those who have great compassion work so hard to relieve the suffering of others. For them, it is the same as their own. The great compensation is that this is so for our joy as well, when we love others the same as ourselves.

Chapter Thirteen
False Pride

What is this false pride that makes us feel more important than others? How does it arise?

These are difficult questions, ones that psychologists, sociologists and theologians have explored over centuries. Without claiming special knowledge or expertise in this area, let me share an observation.

False Pride

As we develop in infancy, parents and others shower us with caring and attention. This is the only way we could ever survive, since we are wholly dependent beings. Other than love and need, there is little else we have to offer at this stage.

These circumstances place us at the center of attention where others put our needs ahead of theirs. It gives us a sense of central importance from the earliest stage of our lives. It is the way we first come to see ourselves as more important than others.

Of course, this is not a bad thing. It is simply part of life.

But, these circumstances soon change. We grow less dependent. We are able to manage more of our needs

False Pride

for ourselves, and the needs of others
compete with our own. We start to be
dislodged from the center, where we
have lived and formed our identities,
the only world we have known.

This transition is never easy.
We experience some cruelty, neglect,
and rejection by others, which twist
our sense of central importance in the
world in ways we cannot understand
or cope with at the time. We begin to
suffer emotional distress.

This challenge to our world
must stimulate a response. We react
to preserve this sense of our central
importance, life as we know it, by a
raw act of will. We adopt false pride,
a feeling that we are more important
than others for no good reason at all,

other than the survival of our initial identity, safe at the center.

What we forget, or never realize, is that everyone else goes through this experience too. We all have this false pride, for the same reason—to protect the world, as we knew it, with us at the center.

This may be nothing more than a case of armchair psychology by an admitted amateur. But it can make a difference in how we regard ourselves ("us") and others ("them") who exhibit this false pride.

It may have bearing on the question of evil; if we see this same basic will to endure in the actions of ourselves and others, twisted by our inevitable encounters with rejection, cruelty, and neglect. We may have a greater compassion and tolerance of our failings with this view.

When I see the behavior of others whose values and attitudes deeply offend me ("them"), it helps me feel more acceptance, humility, and good will in the midst of these important differences to remember that we are similar in our efforts to protect ourselves at the center.

Chapter Fourteen
Healing

Can we heal this false pride? How might it work?

If the condition of false pride arises from being loved and our need for continued love, for importance in the lives of ourselves and others, then it follows that an abundance of love is the power that can heal us. This is the power of God's healing love.

Healing

This healing power can be seen in the image of God's children, as we love and serve each other. We share in this power to heal, by loving one another as ourselves.

The first stage of this love is deep tolerance. If we know we all are afflicted with false pride, and that we do evil because of it, then we begin to understand that we need to bear with each other's weaknesses in life.

This is no trivial task. It can involve great suffering, both to our physical and psychic selves. But, as we realize that all the evil we see in others ("them") stems from roots of seeking for love and self-worth, the same as our own, a new attitude of acceptance and good will arises. We understand that we are the same as them. We all need the same healing release from this false pride.

Our task then becomes to suffer one another's weaknesses, in our bodies and minds, to seek to do good instead of evil, and to seek to relieve our mutual sufferings along the way. We move toward realizing our potential as children of God in the image of God's healing love. We make the world a better place.

As we give and accept this healing love in our lives, feelings of true self-worth begin to remove our false pride from its place. We know the love of God for us in others and for others in us, and we all begin to

Healing

find our identities safely restored at the center, with everyone else.

This is no pipe dream of paradise. It goes on every day. We witness it everywhere in the world. In the midst of great evil, goodness always shines. That is the nature of human being, in the image of God, the children of God on earth.

It does not matter that this process is not yet perfectly complete, or that we may not be able to see the ultimate outcome of this struggle on earth. What matters, is that we know it works. We can prove the power of this healing love for us and others by giving and accepting it.

We see what love, acceptance, and tolerance do for the self-worth of

ourselves and others, as we live with
our differences and suffer the burden
of our mutual failings. These feelings
of self-worth can gradually displace
our defensive false pride as we reach
a point where we realize that it is not
necessary for us to be at the center of
importance by ourselves. We come to
an understanding that self-worth and
love are abundant for all, that it takes
nothing away from us when we share
these with others ("them").

Chapter Fifteen
Idolatry

False pride leads us to serve false gods. This makes perfect sense. We need something false to support that which is false. The true love of God will only destroy it.

False gods can be anything. The more obvious ones come readily to mind: money, power, and prestige. These are where we put our trust and lift ourselves above others to protect our pride, safe at the center.

Of all these false gods, money may be the one most prevalent today. As the medium of exchange, it is how we quantify and store value from our economic activity. Since work is such an important part of life and welfare, money can swiftly be converted into a value in itself. We all are witness to its amazing power in our lives. Those who have money, automatically have great power and prestige.

But, even money can fail. Those who have lived through times of hyperinflation have seen the value of their currency reduced to nothing, their life savings eliminated. At such times, only a new monetary unit can step in to revive the economy.

Also, money cannot always buy the most important things in life. It cannot change that which is within. It has no power to truly love.

This is the basic nature of idolatry, when we devote ourselves to something that can never love us, no matter how we serve. If it cannot love us, it is not God, no matter how much power it may have in life.

Money is not the only thing that cannot love us. An idea cannot love. An institution cannot love. Our most cherished doctrines and sacred texts cannot love. Our specific beliefs and practices cannot love.

Idolatry

Like money, all these things may be means and tokens of power and love, but they are not love itself. God is love. Only the living children of God, in the image of God, can love one another. Sentient beings are the only sources of love in this world; all else are mere instruments. When we worship any object, whether tangible or abstract, this is idolatry.

The most dangerous form of idolatry is when we value our beliefs and practices more than we value the lives and feelings of others. Then our ideas (which are part of "us") become our god, more valuable to us than the children of God, created like us in the image of God, capable of love.

Idolatry

Why is this most dangerous? Because we mistakenly put ourselves (our beliefs and practices) in the place of God, and value our imperfect ideas above the welfare of real beings made in the image of God. If we turn away from God in this manner, how do we return? How can the true God of love get through to us, when our approach itself leads in the wrong direction?

What power is left to help us, when we let our ideas of God become perverted into our reason for denying the equal worth of others ("them")?

Chapter Sixteen
Scripture

Scriptures are at the core of our religious traditions. These hold the testimonies, histories, teachings, and stories of our faiths.

These books are sacred to us believers, containing the words, gifts, and promises of God to the children of God. This is so for our own faiths ("us"), as it is for others ("them").

Scripture

Yet, we see many dark and terrible things in these writings. And, people often understand them in very different ways. How can we reconcile these discrepancies?

Here again, the love of God is our guide. If our understanding of a scripture passage leads us to greater love for God and the children of God, all of "them," then we hear the voice of God in our scriptures.

If we use a scripture passage to justify or support our disrespect or mistreatment of others, then we hear the voice our own false pride, an idol separating us from God.

It is not my place to interpret specific passages for anyone. We can turn to our own teachers and leaders in our own faiths to help us with this challenge. Sometimes, it may take a lifetime or beyond for us to reach an understanding of difficult passages. This is all part of our faith.

But, do not be misled by difficult passages into thoughts or feelings that separate you from the love of God or of the children made in the image of God. Anything that leads us to do good is from God.

Find religious teachers who lead you to do good, and they will guide your understanding of these more difficult passages. Turn away from those who lead you to do evil, even if they tell you it is good.

In turning to good, we are turning to God. This is part of our growing in faith. This growth takes courage, which comes from faith in the love of God, when we trust our own conscience, even if this means we no longer follow teachings that once nurtured us in this faith.

Our scriptures come to us through centuries, from times and places that are different from our own circumstances. But the love of God is the same—yesterday, today, and tomorrow. This is the light we use to guide our understanding of scripture and all things.

None of us have perfect understanding. Neither those who teach us, nor those we teach. This is why our conscience is so important. Just as the scriptures help to inform our consciences, so our consciences can help our understanding of some of the more difficult passages in our scriptures. In addition, we have our faith and humility to help us search for answers as we grow.

If we cannot understand a passage of scripture in a way that increases our love, this shows how much there remains for us to learn about our own faiths.

Chapter Seventeen
Chosen

When we recognize the immensity of God's love for us, it makes us feel great personal worth, safe at the center of attention again, like a newborn child.

We feel somehow special, different, than we were before. We feel that God has "chosen" us, and we sense a calling to fulfill a higher purpose in our lives.

Much good can come from this. It can elevate our motivations and behavior, and lead us to great self-improvement.

However, there is always a risk that these feelings can also lead to great evil. If we fail to grasp that God has "chosen" to love everyone ("them"), the same as us, we fail to appreciate the immensity of God's love to us as the children of God in the image of God.

If we believe that we are "chosen" by ourselves ("us"), and somehow more loved by God than others ("them"), we deny the power of God's love as immense enough to reach the whole of creation. We fall into the false pride of feeling that we are worth more than others.

This is a form of idolatry, when we falsely serve an image of God that is so limited as to love only us. We substitute this image for the love of God, which extends to every being in creation.

This experience of being "chosen" also seems to be held in common across all religious faiths. Believers in every tradition feel the love of God choosing them.

So, here again, we may ask what God is telling us. Could it be that all are "chosen" by God's love? No matter what our background or specific practices and beliefs?

Chosen

What does this tell us about God, and about everyone around us who is "chosen" by this love? Do we see the immensity of God's love? The great worth of everyone we see, who God has "chosen" with this love?

In seeing this, would we not feel truly safe at the center, loved by God and surrounded by others who also share this love? Who would we fear in such a state? Who could ever take away this love?

On the other hand, if we are the only "chosen" ones in our minds ("us"), then we must live in fear that others may usurp this privileged role ("them"). Our worth is not protected by the love of a God that is sufficient to love all of creation.

Chosen

We then require a constant stream of validation of our "chosen" worth, in the form of success, victory, money, acclaim, desire. We are never truly safe at the center, because there is always someone outside the circle of "chosen" love, looking to come in and take our place.

When we see God's love choosing others ("them"), as well as ourselves ("us"), we are truly safe.

Chapter Eighteen
Skepticism

If we step back and consider the great diversity of specific practice and belief among world religions, an open-minded skepticism can become a sincere humble response.

If God is speaking to you, and you, and you—and you hear so many different messages, then what am I to make of all this? For centuries, people dealt with this by saying, "I am right, and they are wrong." This results in a schism (between "us" and "them"), which separates people from each other. Ironically, these are people who share an experience together, that of deep faith.

Under these circumstances, skepticism is not necessarily a sign of a closed mind or disbelieving spirit. It can be the response of an open mind and believing spirit, when faced with such contradictions.

The skeptical person of deep faith might say, "I believe all of you, except where you disagree," and say this with all sincerity.

If God has truly spoken to so many believers, and the messages we hear are so different, then what does this tell us? God is the same. Only we are different. Could it be that we hear the same message in different ways? We know this happens all the time in life, among ourselves. It is difficult to clearly hear what another says. And, this is another human being.

How much more difficult might it be for us to comprehend a message from God? Viewed in this light, it becomes remarkable that we find so much in common as we do in the different world religions.

It is to this common ground, which the skeptical open mind and believing spirit turn. We turn to the core message of God's love. All else may involve nothing more than our human weaknesses and limitations, and different circumstances.

Of course, we still believe what we believe; this is the definition of the word. And, others believe what they believe as well. Is it possible that this diversity is perfectly acceptable, and even pleasing, to God?

After all, if we all believe the same things, what do we learn from each other? It is in our differences, as well as our common core truths, that we find a more glorious aspect of the immensity of God's love.

You hear one thing. I hear another. Some things, we both hear the same. Let us share what we hear, that all may be nurtured.

Skepticism

The more we know about other people, the more we know about ourselves. The more we see other views of God, the better we come to see our own.

Skepticism is a natural and beneficial result of diversity (of "us" and "them"), when met with an open mind and believing spirit. Skepticism is not the enemy of faith. It is its best friend, the fertile ground in which it is cultured and grown.

Chapter Nineteen
Children

As believers, we think of human beings as the children of God. In part, this is because we see God as our creator, the giver of life. It is also because we understand the love of a parent for his or her child, which we relate to God's love for us.

In addition, some see in this label a reference to us being made in

the image of God, with a capacity to
magnify this image in our beings, as
we grow in Divine love. For all this,
there is yet another dimension to this
concept. It has to do with the limited
stage of our development relative to
the immensity of God's love.

Compare the humanity of an
infant to that of its parents. An infant
is made in the image of its parents. It
looks like them, and over many years
will grow to become like them, fully
developed adult human beings.

Still, the infant has none of
their powers. The infant cannot do
much of anything on its own power.
It cannot feed, clothe, shelter, bathe,
or care for itself in this world, not to
mention doing this for another.

Children

Infants cannot comprehend the world of adults. They live in our homes, structures they did not build. The foundations, walls, roofs, ducts, and utilities are beyond the grasp of their limited experience. They are not even aware of the neighborhoods and vast world beyond their dwellings. In fact, they know practically nothing at all beyond themselves, their primitive needs, their immediate families, and the love they share with others.

Even as they progress to the toddler stage, and can walk on their own two feet and begin to learn our language, they still are infinitely far from comprehending the vast and intricate world of adults. They have practically no experience compared to adults. They have no power.

Imagine or remember how large and confusing the world is to young children. They simply do not comprehend this world at all. They lack any frame of reference to place themselves in the world in any way that makes full sense to them.

So it is with us, if we think about the bigger picture of this life and our place in it. Even with all of our advances in modern science, we still do not grasp the immensity and intricacy of this world. We remain as children living in a house we did not build and do not comprehend.

Likewise, even those who live among us with a great power of love compared with others, fall infinitely short of the immensity of God's love. They are like older children, toddlers among infants, teaching the rest of us how to crawl, and maybe walk, in the love of God. These are our saints.

God gives them to us among all religions, one the same as another. In view of this bounty, who can say that one religion is right and another wrong? When the fruits of God's love are found among all of them.

Chapter Twenty
Humanity

Do our religious faiths help us to be better human beings? Not better than others, but better than we would be ourselves without these faiths.

Are we more kind, merciful, compassionate, humble, tolerant, and giving than we would be without our faiths? The value of a faith is not how it stokes our zeal toward the idea of a

---

Humanity

God we cannot see. Rather, the value of faith is how it leads us to a greater love for the children of God, where we can see the image of God.

Sometimes, when we first experience the power of God's love, we can be so overwhelmed that we temporarily lose sight of others. We think about ourselves and God, and the love we have found, and we can forget to think about anyone else. It becomes intensely personal.

In these times, we are most susceptible to false pride, idolatry, and a notion of being chosen above others ("us" over "them"). This is a normal part of the faith experience, much as a child feels itself to be the center of attention in its world. We have these imperfections, and they come out in these circumstances, as they do in other areas of our lives. It is all part of our common experience as we grow in our faiths.

However, as we encounter others and learn from this diversity, we begin to see God's love is so great that it extends to everyone (to "them" as well as to "us"). This gives way to humility and healthy skepticism with respect to the exclusive merits of our specific practices and beliefs.

Our conscience grows more fully informed by needs and values of others ("them") outside our own narrow experience ("us"). We begin to hear God calling us to compassion, service, and celebration of others, the same as ourselves. We see the image of God in everyone we meet.

This is when we fully realize that we all are children of God. None of us are adults. We all are nurtured in the love of God, as a child lives by the love of its parents. We all depend on this love for everything.

We then begin to realize our full humanity. Our religious faiths, which may have divided us before, now bring us together in a common experience of God's love. We find in the beliefs and practices of others the same exercise of faith that we find in our own, even though we are able to believe in our own as before.

God has spoken to people throughout the millennia, over the

whole world. The core of all these messages is the same—to love and serve each other as children of God, revealing the image of God.

This is Divinity. Everything else is us—receiving the message of God's love in specific circumstances, subject to our own limitations. Now is the time for us to learn from these differences, to let them bring people together, not tear us apart.

Please visit the website for this book, w*ww.InterfaithJourney.com.*

At the website, readers can ask questions and receive answers from leaders and ministers of the religious traditions that richly bless our lives, based on the principles in this book.

We deepen our own faith as we broaden our appreciation for the different faiths of others. Let us share in the peace of this InterfaithJourney, walking separate paths together.